simple machines

Screws

RIGBY
INTERACTIVE
LIBRARY

David Glover

This edition © 1997 Rigby Education
Published by Rigby Interactive Library,
an imprint of Rigby Education,
division of Reed Elsevier, Inc.
500 Coventry Lane,
Crystal Lake, IL 60014

Printed in Hong Kong / China

01
10 9 8 7 6 5 4 3

Library of Congress Cataloging-in-Publication Data
Glover, David, 1953 Sept. 4–
    Screws/David Glover.
        p. cm.—(Simple machines)
    Includes index.
    Summary: Introduces the principles of screws as simple machines, using examples from everyday life.
    ISBN 1–57572–085–X (lib. bdg.)
    1. Screws—Juvenile literature. [1. Screws.] I. Title.
II. Series: Glover, David, 1953 Sept. 4– Simple machines.
TJ1338.G48 1997
621.8 ' 82—dc20
                                       96-15800
                                         CIP
                                       AC

Designed by Celia Floyd and Sharon Rudd
Illustrations by Barry Atkinson (pp. 5, 15, 17, 18, 23) and Douglas Hall (p. 11)

Acknowledgments
The publisher would like to thank the following for permission to reproduce photographs:
Trevor Clifford, pp. 4, 6, 7, 8, 9, 10, 11, 14, 18, 20, 21; Robert Harding Picture Library, p. 12; Zefa, pp. 13, 17; Trip/J Ringland, p. 15; Spectrum Colour Library, p. 22.

Cover photograph by Trevor Clifford

Every effort has been made to contact copyright holders of any material reproduced in this book. Any omissions will be rectified in subsequent printings if notice is given to the publisher.

> **Note to the Reader**
> Some words in this book are printed in **bold** type. This indicates that the word is listed in the glossary on page 24. This glossary gives a brief explanation of words that may be new to you and tells you the page on which each word first appears.

Contents

What Are Screws?

A screw is a cone-shaped machine with a **groove** that winds round and round it in a spiral. The groove is called a **thread**. When a carpenter turns a wood screw, the thread cuts into the wood. With each turn, the screw is pulled either into or out of the wood. After several turns, the screw is either firmly in place or out of the wood.

one turn

spiral thread

forward movement

A screw can overcome resistance with little energy. By winding the screw in a little at a time, a person can drive it into the wood with little effort.

With screws, people can tighten and grip things with much more force than they can by pushing or pulling.

FACT FILE

Screw strength

All the effort a person uses to turn a screw is focused into small turns inward. A screw makes a small bit of effort go a long way.

Lids and Caps

This soda bottle has a screw cap. The cap fits tightly enough to keep the gas bubbles in the soda from escaping. If you forget to screw the cap back on tightly after pouring a drink, the soda will lose its bubbles, or go flat.

When closed, the cap presses a small circle of plastic onto the neck of the bottle. This **seals** the bottle and keeps in the bubbles.

Screw caps on jars help to keep food fresh. They seal tightly enough to stop **germs** from getting into the jar. They also stop the food inside from drying out.

FACT FILE

Screws in History

The screw is one of six simple machines that have existed since ancient times. The others are the lever, the wheel and axle, the pulley, and the ramp, and the wedge.

Nuts and Bolts

Nuts and **bolts** work together to connect things. A bolt is a metal rod with a head at one end and a screw thread at the other. A nut is a chunk of metal with a hole in the middle. The thread on a bolt screws into the thread inside a nut.

A wrench is used to tighten a nut. It can help make a nut so tight that it holds the wheels on a bike.

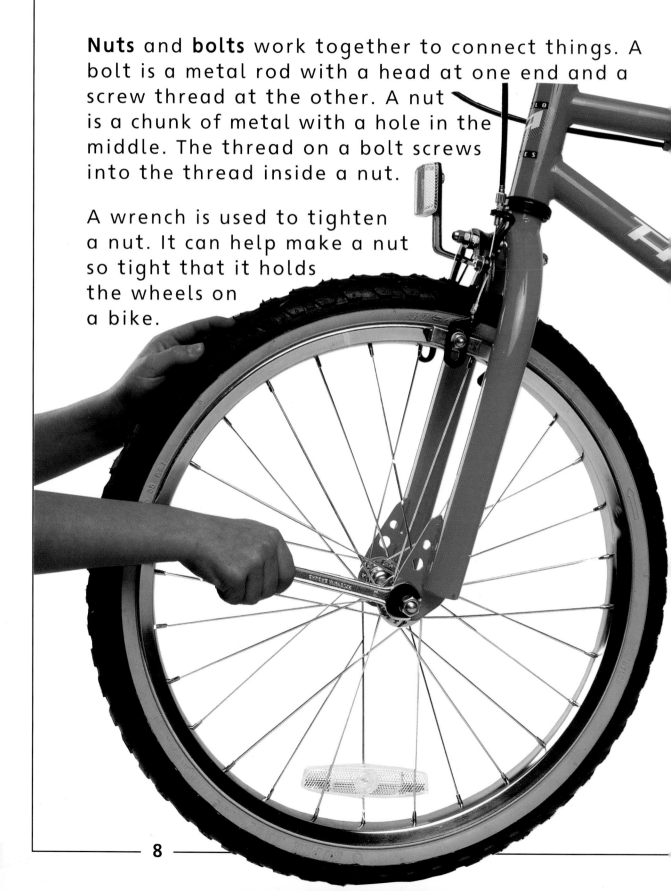

Nuts come in different shapes and sizes. The most common shape is a *hexagon,* which has six sides. Some nuts are wing-shaped and can be turned with the fingers. Others are square.

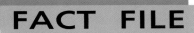

FACT FILE

Wrench Power!

More energy is used to turn a large wrench than a small one, so added energy is focused on the screw's turns. This helps make the screw tighter.

Corkscrews and Drills

As it turns,
it winds slowly
into the cork like
a screw, gripping
it tightly enough
for it to be pulled
out.

A drill is used to bore holes into things. Some drills turn a thin steel rod called a *drillbit*. The drillbit has a spiral thread which winds waste material back from the hole.

An **auger** is a huge drill used to make big holes for tasks like planting trees. The auger has a wide thread that winds the soil out of the hole.

drillbit

Staircases and Slides

A spiral staircase is like a giant screw that people climb. They move up higher each time they make a full turn. The spiral spreads energy needed for climbing over a long distance. This means that each step up takes less effort than when people climb straight up.

A spiral slide is great fun! Gravity, the force that makes things fall, pulls you down the slide. The spiral spins you around. Some water slides use the same idea, except at the end, you land with a big splash!

FACT FILE

Which Way Around?

Spiral staircases nearly always go up *clockwise*. This means that as you go up the stairs, you turn in the same direction that the hands on a clock turn.

Tops and Propellers

When the knob of this top is pushed down, a screw thread inside the top turns. This, in turn, makes the top spin.

The **propellers** on airplanes are sometimes called *props* or *air screws*. The **blades** are twisted so that they pull the plane through the air as they turn. They screw through the air like a wood screw pushing into wood.

FACT FILE

Tree spinners

The seeds of maple trees have wings that work like propellers. They spin around as they fall.

Water Screws

An Archimedes screw is a kind of **water pump.** It moves water from one place to another. The turning screw of the pump winds water up from a lower level to a higher one.

FACT FILE

Ancient screws

Archimedes of ancient Greece invented the Archimedes screw more than 2,000 years ago. The Archimedes screw is a kind of pump that farmers in some countries still use today.

The propeller on this boat is a water screw. As the blades spin, they push water backward. This makes the boat move forward, just as a propeller pushes back air and makes a plane move forward.

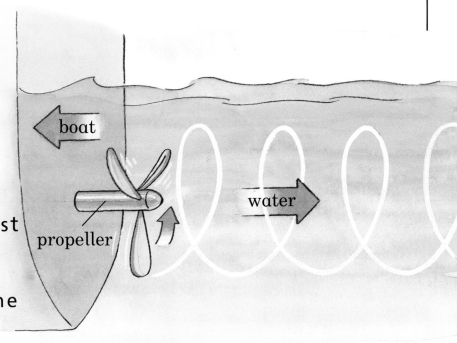

Hoses and Faucets

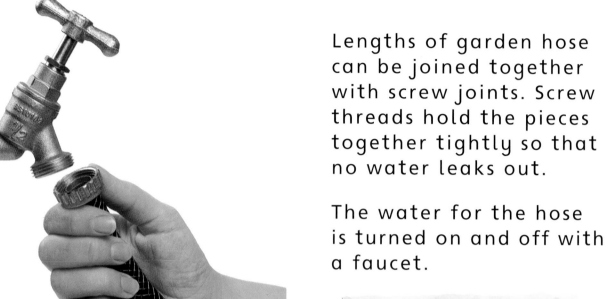

Lengths of garden hose can be joined together with screw joints. Screw threads hold the pieces together tightly so that no water leaks out.

The water for the hose is turned on and off with a faucet.

The screw inside the faucet exaggerates the force from your fingers as you turn it. The screw moves a **washer** up or down. The washer blocks or unblocks the hole the water flows through.

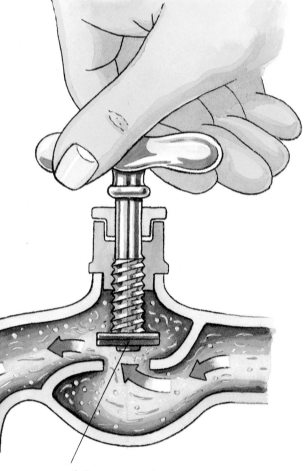

rubber washer

FACT FILE

Water Pressure

A faucet works hard to stop water
from flowing out. If you turned on
a hose and blocked the end with your
thumb, water would squirt everywhere!

Jacks and Clamps

Can a person lift a car with bare hands? Mechanics can—by using a screw jack, which is a screw combined with a lever. When the screw is turned, the lever is raised. The car rises a little at a time.

A screw jack holds a car up just long enough to change a tire. Never get underneath a car that is on a jack!

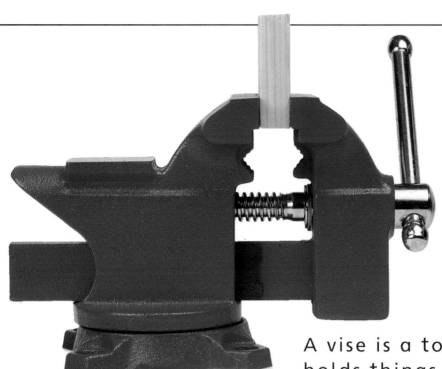

A vise is a tool that holds things firmly for sawing, bending, and hammering. A screw moves the jaws of the vise closer together.

A C-clamp is a vise-like tool that holds parts together while glue dries. C-clamps come in many sizes, from tiny to huge.

Tunnel Borers

How do you dig a tunnel under water? You dig it with a tunnel borer, a machine that cuts through the rock like a giant drill.

Tunnel-boring machines are like giant drills. They have spinning blades at the front. As the machine is pushed forward, the blades cut into the rock. The cut rock passes back through holes in the blades. It is taken out of the tunnel by train.

The Channel Tunnel goes under the sea between England and France. It took eleven huge tunnel-boring machines six years to build it.

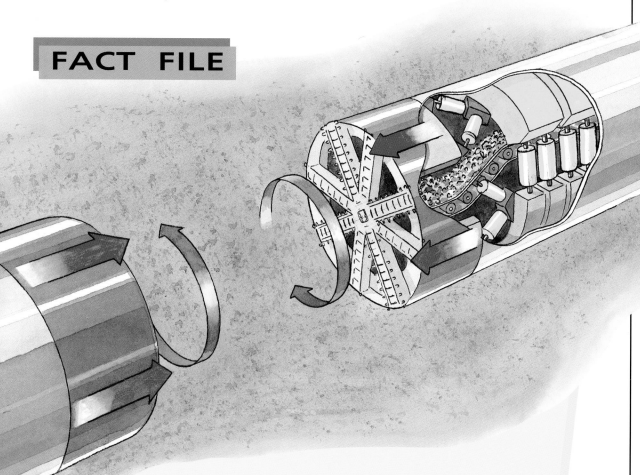

Perfect match!

Machines started the Channel Tunnel from both ends at the same time. The machines moved forward about three feet each hour. The two halves of the tunnel lined up perfectly when the machines met in the middle.

Glossary

auger   Huge drill used to make large holes   **11**

blade   The sharp cutting part of a knife   **15**

bolt   A type of screw used with a nut, for holding things together   **8**

germs   Microorganisms that can cause disease   **7**

grooves   Long narrow channel, cut into something   **4**

nut   Metal chunk that screws onto the end of a bolt to hold things together   **8**

propellers   Blades that spin around to pull a plane through the air or push a boat through water   **15**

seal   To close an object very tightly   **6**

thread   The spiral groove around a bolt or screw   **4**

washer   A flat ring used in joints to prevent leaks or tighten seals   **18**

water pump   A machine for raising water up from deep in the ground   **16**

wrench   A tool used for turning a bolt   **8**

Index

More Books to Read

Barton, Bryon. *Machines at Work*. New York: Harper Collins, 1987.

Stine, Megan. *Hands-On Science: Fun Machines*. Milwaukee: Gareth Stevens, 1993.